Turquoise Silence

Sanober Khan

"For my Aunts".

Contents

Poetry In My Heart

When poetry
finds my heart

I am suddenly
the empress of the world

I sleep as a rock
and wake up as a mountain

I pause as a seed
and burst into silk floss trees

I stream through silence
ripple into whispers, and swell into a song

I begin as a single snowflake
and end in an avalanche

life continually flows
through my fingertips,
like fortune through a talisman

I am suddenly vulnerable
and invincible all at once

I blink January's lashes
and gush down December's cheeks

I float as an orphan
and descend with family wings

I wait by solitude's window
and then flee,
like confetti in the winds

I touch with material hands
and feel with a Sufi's soul

I take birth as a mortal
and die...
as an immortal

I am infinitely yearning,
brimming...overflowing,
in words

and I discover, it's another way
for me...to be in tears

Tonight's Moon

Tonight's moon...is just the kind of moon
that i had been hoping for

the full-orbed, incandescent pearl
against a Turkish eye-blue sky

with the creamy haloed breath,

with a few curious children
of clouds, flitting over to see
what all the mystique is about

with some stars dusted in
for good measure

tonight's moon...is just the moon
that makes the sleeping birds,
look like treasures,

and the ocean...
full of silver-inked love poems,

the kind that always tips me over,
into magical realms
folklores, and parables,
childhood and cherry blossoms

the kind that would go well
with hot chocolate, or sweet wine
nostalgia or grief,

the moon that...
softens gazes, and smoothens hands
and steers feet,
that have nowhere to go

the kind of moon
that I'd boast around
to my solitude

kiss upon my pillow,
and squeeze to my chest
like a precious pet

the kind that I would want to
to send back to my ancestors
and gift to my descendants

so they know that I too,
have been bruised...by beauty,

the kind of moon...that just aches
to be touched...with poetry

the moon... that I want to
gaze up at, until my neck begins to hurt,
and heels begin to crack,

until my eyes cannot take in..
something so heartbreakingly beautiful
anymore

the moon that I want to...
press my cheek against
and cry.

Beautiful Moment

Today...you are just a wraith
upon the winds...

oh Beautiful Moment!

just a wraith...

a mere flashlight
...of a kiss

a vanishing steam
off my heart's coffee

a mere blink,
of babyhood

you are perhaps...

the Sunday mornings
syruping down my toast

the blush of summer's cheeks
watering down...to a photograph

the lingering grace of a gazelle..
in an empty savannah

you are...
as fleetingly beautiful

as a mother's tears,
and a father's pranks

a brother's bachelorhood
and a best friend's bad mood

a bride's glittering jitters
and a handsome stranger's smile

you are perhaps...
the long-haired,
ageless copper red beauty
disappearing...into the horizon

wing-marks left in the sky
by a favorite bird

memories...
puffing away
at the soul's cigarette

simply passing...
like my name
upon time's misty lips

today, you may just be

a vapour

tomorrow,
you will be a poem.

Those Words

They have been whispered...
for centuries, and handed down...generations

endorsed by sunrises, sunsets
and embodied under thunderstorms

fruited on winter trees...
and chanted by chocolates,

forested...
by faith

those same words...
now resounding...in my ear,

...

Don't lose heart

Greetings

I could greet you, my dear
with a huge, cupcake smile on my face

with butterfly flutters, in my hair
and summer clouds, in my arms

with presents and gifts,
and a lemonade kiss,
for your lips,

i could arrange for the whole city...to rejoice
in the festival...of your return,
with a heaven-spun feast

or i could greet you.... with a shriek

loud and excited enough, to interrupt...
the blissful wheeling of the seagulls

or with a gasp,
softer than a baby's skin

or with a sickeningly
sweet, fluffy giggle

with a whoopee dance,
that would put ballerinas to shame

or with a deep and warm
blueberry sigh,

or i could welcome you
with the impatience,
of a melting ice cream

with the nimble capering
of balloons in the air

or with a touch so...gentle
it would make dewdrops...
feel insecure

but you deserve more, my dear

so i will greet you
...in a way
all loved things
are meant to be greeted

with a tear in my heart
and a poem in my eye.

Natural Cures

Lusciously unfolded
true-blue skies
for lackluster eyes..

lemon-fresh grass...
for the throbbing feet

a breath of birdsong
for overburdened shoulders

sea-spun winds
for dampened cheeks

reveries of warm tea
for the melancholy heart

and the balm of poetry
for the aching soul.

What's a rainy day

What's a rainy day,
without some longing...in the eyes

without some languor
in between...huge, fluffy pillows,

and some delicious
coffee-flavoured loneliness?

is it anything at all... without children
bursting...into a dance of paradise

without tarmacs glistening
like a bride's necklace

without the endearing sight...of birds
fluffing their plumage

and without a romance novel
to curl up with?

oh is it anything at all
without the shimmering promise
of rainbows

without some nostalgia
fogging up the windows

without a serenade in the heart,
and thirst in the fingertips

without the melancholic
sway of the soul?

Is it anything
without the old rain coat
of bittersweet memories

without the mystic murmurings
of poetry in the ear

and without an afterglow
from within?

Oh what's a rainy day…

it's nothing….

nothing

nothing

without you

and it's simply nothing…without me

The Good Times (Memories of Khandala)

We couldn't hold on
to the rain-flowers of those times, forever
not with our hands, certainly

when we slipped down,
moss-whiskered rocks

watched the swish
and sailing-away of moments
through shoddily made
paper bombs and paper boats

lamely attempted
to catch tadpoles
in bathroom mugs

all those mornings,
we passed by fresh waterfalls,
and someone always mumbled
they're called 'cataracts'
and not waterfalls

watched the chilly fog
drink us all in…sip by sip

invented our own
family national game…
"Football Cricket"

savoured the long drive to Sunny's dhaba...
to binge on butter-bathed
garlic *naans* and chicken *tikka's,*
sarson ka saags, and *lassi's*
when we never had to worry about cellulite,
belly fat...and love handles,

all those luxuriously slow strolls,
along Summer Hill mountain's ridge
the swirl of mosquitoes,
and ghost stories at night

all the pranks we played...
with those horror masks

it seemed forgettable...back then

but we always knew,
that good times came
with termination contracts,
even if we weren't quite ready,
to sign it

when we watched,
our beautiful holiday home
turn into a topic
for brokers and buyers and sellers

it saddens me today
for we couldn't hang on

for those memories are now
just like these little kittens,
I hold in my hands

those can be kissed,
and treasured
but not held too tightly.

The Rain at 4 A.M

It's different
the rain at 4 am
purer...
somehow
more tender-hearted

like silvery sprigs
being gently garnished...
upon my window

a dish for the soul...

unlike the rain at 4 pm
when the shoreline
is as wild...as the curls
of the bleached-haired girl,
standing amongst a swarm
of merrymakers and hooligans

disrupting my view,
of the Arabian sea...

with the sky...
dunking its greyness
into the cup of me, whipping up
inordinate amounts,
of melancholia

which makes me shiver,

with zip-zapping cars
muddying my pants
and cell phone
and cheeks

i've actually always preferred
the rain...as it is right now,
silently musical, at 4 am
unleashed,
yet restrained,

when I am more than content
to stay curled in bed,
as much as I'd love...
to lap up the rain

because some things,
sometimes

aren't ours to hold,

but just beautiful
to listen to.

Ungrateful

It would be best to term me
as the ungrateful one,
a terminal grouch,
hopelessly incurable...

forever whining
that i cannot cup the stars
against my face,
whisper...in their ear,
a name...that tickles my lips

that i cannot fly away
with the seagulls, high-five the skies
like the tide at noon,

that I cannot comfort
a romance novel's handsome,
heartbroken hero, touch his cheek. . .

cannot make my home
in a robin's nest,
stay curled and cosied
and chocolated....forever,
in my mother's arms,

for i cannot always make autumn
walk beside me like a friend,

and make the moon, kiss-soothe
my worn out shoulders at all times,

for daddy won't always be
strong enough to do
a thousand crunches every day,
and Princes won't always be
all that charming,

for I won't always be lucky
to make sure everyone's safely
tucked away for the night

for all I can really do is, stand here
in September's rain, savoring…
soaking it all in..
slipping, and simply
holding on to poetry, for dear life.

Moments

Someday these moments
will come again

marked, unmistakably
with the passage of time

smelling of
family festivities
and friendship's hot cocoas
seaweed evenings...
mom-made warmth,

they'll come
burrowing beside me

to whisper...

and cradle

to sing,

to comfort,

to haunt.

Once in a While

Once in a while i am struck
all over again... by just how blue
the sky appears .. on wind-played
autumn mornings, blue enough

to bruise a heart, by how sweet
the chirping sparrows sound,
against my fluffy pillow,

by how my day fills up..
with merry vibes, when begun
with a sun-sized smile and breakfast,

how magically a butter cookie
melts in my mouth

sometimes i stand in front of the
mirror, marveling at how strongly
my eyes... resemble my dad's

at my shoulders...only as broad
as my paternal aunt's would allow,

at how my hair turn...into a breathtaking
shade of burnt umber and burgundy,
in the brush of daylight,
at the speedy changes, in time's tempo,
in people's promises, attitudes, and interests

in the elegiac mystique,
in a certain pair of eyes,

at the timeless beauty... in my mother's face,
the warmth and fuzziness that emanates ...from a
a good old laugh and classic love stories,
at the ever beguiling fragrance
found only...in a bottle of J'adore,
I am filled...time and again…

with a heart-aching wonder when I think
of the fire and frost ….of memories...
of the everlastingness
of love, the solace of family...
and the power of prayer.

Pursuit of Comfort

I could lie starfish-spread
in the sands for hours
just lie there until...
twilight comes

or until my sadness... begins to float..
into soap bubbles
and balloons

until my soul is permanently
perfumed with the sea...

or maybe I could sit beside
an old friend, in an old park, pouring myself
in alternating flower-bursts
of joys and sorrows....

I could just sing
until the tragic opera music
of my heart....blossoms
into a blissful ballad of the 90's

melt into marshmallows..
and dark chocolate and coffee
until my only worry
...is the calories I'm consuming

wrap myself...onto the rain
in jubilation and remembrance
and mourning...of what's gone

or just allow my own solitude,
to be my truest companion

but for the greatest
comfort of all...I could just wait...
until the world is tucked in...for the night
until the moon... is cool
on my cheeks
and then quietly, caress...
a stranger's poem...in my arms
and whisper, '*You just saved my life*'.

Rain Blue Eyes

I wish to stay drenched
forever....in those rain-blue eyes

...in those…soul-reaching crystals....

not moving a muscle,
nor breathing,
just...
savoring...
this turquoise ache,
against my heart...

this molten affection...

this delicious ...
devastation

this tearful..
tenderness

this longing's kiss
with parted lips.

Some Poems

There are some poems that lie hidden
in the wings of birds…like secret
melodies, only to be revealed…each ruffled
feather by feather

there are some, that are scattered…
all across the horizon…
in sun-glimmers, and violin-winds

some froth and foam and rise...
out of my morning cup of
mist-sweetened coffee,

some drift...in dreamy wisps
from between the pages...
of a favourite book

some are laden...
in the deep, chocolate-rich
songster's voice, some perpetually
embedded...in turquoise eyes,
and a tousle...of brown hair

while some poems wait, like
mountain peaks...enshrouded
in the distance

some smolder on the beams
of my own, adoring gaze

some lie drenched...
even before my own tears
have fallen, and some remain clenched...
eternally, in the chest

and then
there are some poems..
that we leave behind
some that leave us behind

while some just live... silently,
in the heart, crumble...sometimes
dwindle, disappear...die

and are reborn
when you smile again.

Let Me Die

When you're going to kill me, anyway
oh life ....then let me die

from having being drunk on
indigo skies, my liver...
overflowing with stars

from having a sudden
moonstroke, right there...
in my 7th floor balcony
with no ambulance on the way

from cuddling my blanket
...a little too tight

from breathing in the sea scent
in illegally high dosages

let me turn into a
diabetic...from the saccharine
whisperings of ancient love stories,
kisses on my forehead

from the overwhelmingly
bittersweet memory,
of last year's holiday

from having savored
too much poetry,
too much coffee

let my arteries stay blocked,
with butterflies and bluebirds
and beachside days,

let my hands begin
to quiver and weaken...but only because
they once filled yours

or let me just die...

from having gazed at you,
too long

from a cancer...
of unbearable love

from the merciless, violent assault
of all this beauty,
that my heart just couldn't take.

Slipping

There you go…Oh another day
sagging....into yesterday's arms,
silently... being washed off teacups,
and smoothed from beds,

dusted off photo-frames,
and curtained away...
from my eyes

into another morning
sweated away...
another afternoon...
dipped in drowse..

into another evening...
immersed in the warm tea memory
of the thousands...preceding it,
of the ones... yet to follow

shriveling
into yet another
number...on the calendar

relinquishing
in the hands
of the ancient clockworks
with no ceremony...

for our parting, no forehead kiss...
no warm, quick embrace

always...
silently slipping

like a grandparent
passing away... in their sleep

All Things Past

Sometimes

all i have left to offer life

is a wistful gaze,
cast across the ocean

a sad little smile,
and drooping shoulders

a bittersweet sigh,
an empty handshake,
and a prayer,

a tenderly raw ache

for all things past.

Forever Wish List

Give me...
a blush of birds,
for monochrome mornings
such as these

a pair of
tenderly skilled hands
that I can fry eggs, and brew
the coffee of love with..

a touch of jasmines
to refresh me

a yawn of lusciously
blue skies...to inspire me

a pillow of strong
ever-dependable shoulders,
that i can bury my head in

a purse of lips,
that i can always trust
with all my secrets

a symphony
of a deep, sonorous voice
to make me yearn
yet...fulfill me

a cascade of words
to heal me

a rhythm of
high heel-ensconced feet
that I can dance and giggle with

a plane of open palms...
that i can entrust... my life upon

Or just give me....
a moon-blanket night
to keep me warm

a long-gone smile,
to comfort me

a pair of rain-blue eyes
...to haunt me

a simple soul
...to love me.

Some Things

Some roses will only bloom
in the dreams ...of
a dying bud

some moments
will only linger...
in fading cadences
and sighing sunsets

some winters,
will never melt

some summers
we'll never freeze

and some things will only
... live in poems.

Like a Winter Morning

Come to me...like a silent
winter's mist,
on Sunday mornings...

softly seeping...
through the window

savoring
...with me...

the lushness
of a lingering sleep....
and last night's...
dream ...

on coffee-scented wings

cocooning me...
nurturing me...
nourishing…
gently awakening
but never..

breaking the spell.

Midnight

Long after i have slipped...deep...
into my midnight-sparkled bed, i position
myself in such a way, so my body lies

directly, parallel...to the sky,
with the window, just a blush open...curtains
drawn away,.. so the moon appears to be
resting, on the wings ...
of my brow...

so if i hold..
my palms out...i can almost feel...
the shift in the winds, and change...
in constellations, the rise and fall
in the city's chest

clearly hear...the music
in my mother's breathing,
and the dreams... in my father's snoring
...and October's fading laughter....

so if i reach out...
just a little further ...i can almost
touch you...almost...
almost... lace my fingers ...
through yours...
whisper, in your ear...

almost sweep you
away....in the ebb
and flow of me

so even if i toss
and turn, unable to dream, i'm still cast ...
in the sapphires and diamonds
and cool-wind tugs of you

so when I finally begin to drift
into sleep, your memory is the...first
and the moonlight
the last, to kiss my face.

This Winter

This winter, there will be no voices, no glimpses,
no arms...only the fabric of poetry, to keep me warm.

My Moment

All I'll probably need is an old t-shirt
and tracks, disheveled hair, and a steady
stream of inside jokes, to celebrate...
my *moment of madness*

a cup of hot chocolate, and sea-winter
winds, with a haunting tune swelling
through my earphones,
for my *moment of luxury*

i might require a classic novel, too,
the company of cousins, on a weekend
long trip to the hills, to evade
my *moment of monotony*

in search of my heart-lightning
moment of inspiration

a night sky, swishing with
shooting stars and silhouettes...
of flying bats, for my *moment of wonder*

a window overlooking a
rocky valley, reverberating...
with the sound of train horns
for my *moment of melancholy*

and then i will need...a living room
filled with warm amber lights, festive
aromas, and familiar faces, brought even closer...
for my *moment of bliss*

a lavender-vanilla scented
candle, hand woven quilt,
and a whispered...book of poetry,
to savour.... my *moment of longing*

an impromptu long drive
through a moonlit, deserted highway...
for my *moment of adventure*

and mother's shoulders
for my *moment of slumber*

an empty, worn-down shoreline,
echoing with the call ...
of a solitary seagull, joining in
my *moment of mourning*

a winter sun breaking
through a cluster of soul-bare
trees...for my *moment of beauty*

and a quiet place... that no one knows
where i can just slump down...and lie,
weeping... among flowers, in

my *moment of deliverance.*

You Drift

You drift like a haunting melody..
through the winter-greying
streets of me

swelling...
against my heart,

without a word,
nor pause....nor a glance

your memory-like silhouette
cutting a swathe…
through the million wisps

of morning lights...

and mists....

and me

In My Corner

Leave me to roost in some
corner, of this silently

magical night, of this ...

silently...magical place,

where i can savor,
uninterrupted, ...the twirl of its
star-poppied skies...
with long...luxurious blinks

its silhouettes of..
sultana-colored mountains...
seeping...
into my soul

where i can feel the
pulse ...of its distant oceans..
rising to a ...heart-aching crescendo

far away...from the lights
of the city, whispers...
of clocks, and ruffle..
of calendars

where the stillness
of its cornfields..becomes
the dancing dervish in me

and the afterglow...
of your gaze...is the only
sweater that i need

where i can just ..bask
and heal....in that magical silence

when ..
the sudden call of the...
red-wattled lapwing bird

leaves me feeling ....like

every other...sorrow,
beauty, song...
loss...
wonder...
miracle

i have never truly recovered from.

Untouched

I've held you in the palm of my hands, dear life
yet, you long..
to be touched

unmarked..from years
of turning and twisting,... your pages,
still blooming...with the cheeks
of innocence,

rings of desires
circle...the planet of your eyes

oh look! how my feet
long to trace the sand ...
of unwalked beaches,

how my lips..quiver,
from the weight of...
unsung songs, untasted coffees,
unkissed feathers

my fingers lie fanned...
in the hope of catching
years of... unfallen snow

how these gardens ....ache
from all the Junes...still left to bloom,

and how these words, wait to die
in the arms of all the poetry..
yet to be written

oh look!...how this heart yearns...
for the salt of unsmelt air
unswept thunderstorms...

unknown adventures...

for the caress...
of the unblemished,
the unseen...the unfelt...

brimming with the tears... of all
still left to love

and yet...oh time, if you were to
stop....in your tracks
...and linger here,

forever,
please, let this be it...

while mother is still young...
and father can still dance...

on this long journey
fragranced with the petals...

of pristine love.

Every Moment

Every moment
must have a soundtrack

of violins...pianos,
and winds...

every touch...
an eternal festival

every heart....its private
bestseller book

every smile ...
a profound admirer,

every gaze,
a celebration

every whisper,
an endless summer

and every kiss,

a poem.

What does it matter

What does it matter how a moment
arrives, the fanfare...
the proclamations
...or the promises,

or how long...or briefly, it lasts,

when all i can really think about is...

what i'm left with...
in the end

the lingering wonderment...
long after I've watched ...
the spectacle
of meteor showers

the swirling soft, warm glow
in the sweet absence...
of a dearly loved one

the whispering sea-breeze
kiss of serenity... after its shores..
and sands and starfish ...
have long... passed me by

the lilting reverie...
months after i have recovered
from a handsome smile

when it's all...
i can hold on to...

to the solace... left behind
long after the music has faded

the aching...tenderness
towards the wounded bird,
even after it has healed...
and flown away

the dewdrop wistfulness...
after the good times have long
come to an end

to the swelling...sense of
fulfillment...from the knowledge
of a day well-spent, well-loved...

to every...melting warmth
echoing...enchantment..
long after those moment have passed...

what does it matter...

when all i can think about is...

how every farewell... left me

with a clenched heart.

and how the cascading rain left me

with kissed hands.

February Romance

Waking up to sweet-berried
mornings.... in my arms

to having late afternoons
gently..
brush my lips

to waffle-warm evenings
that go perfectly..
with my soul's ...brewed coffee

to having clear riviera nights..
grow misty.... with love

and someone ....
to miss.

Satin visions

Amid satin visions
of moon-cocooned oceans...
i want to ponder
all the wonders...
of life, the heart-piercing
... beauty, the sacredness
of pain

the bottomless
depths and wisdom
of words...

all the miracles..
and love's tenderness

whilst spilling...
into the kind of silence
only Khalil Gibran would understand.

Midnight Prayer

Let my gaze always.. be gentle
gentle....as i would lay a blanket
on a sleeping baby

let my spoken words always
be soft...harmless,
a blunt knife spreading
marmalade...on the toast
of another's life....

my promises....
a sun-fresh farm ...in the southlands,
forever ...in their harvesting season

my touch...always tender...
as i would stroke... mother's cheek
when she cried

my embrace...always warm, eternal
as i would hold on to a life
that was slipping away...

let my own tears...be like
each precious strand of saffron.....
that someone might keep

my journey through each moment
as i would look up in wide-eyed

wonder... at the desert sky,
laugh among friends..dance
in front of the mirror

my faith...at the end of the day
a hummingbird...returning
to its favorite flower

let my heart always be
like it is...this very moment
ready to explode...with love

a violent rainstorm...
with no stream
no ocean vast enough
to flow into.

Picture Perfect Afternoon

It must have been the glow
of the mango warm, afternoon sun,
seeping in, through the drawn curtains,

that suddenly made me
stop in my tracks, and wish

that every afternoon of life
could be like this,

with father relishing
such a heartily full stomach
that he must not be allowed
a nap for at least an hour

and mother bumbling around
with frizzy hair, leaving a scented
trail of Lorea'l shampoo and
fresh laundry,

with my brother sprawled
on the sofa, watching random
movies running on television

the windowsill sprinkled with a few
fluffy pigeons, waiting to be fed

the air around me,
all snugly and sleepy

and with me, mentally
bingeing on donuts, whilst gazing out
at the wildly glittering sea,

just standing there...
with my arms open...and embracing
the world with all its sins and flaws,

at utter peace, with myself,
as though forgiving an old friend.

Tell Me

Tell me of a sweeter nectar
than the liquid surge
of nostalgic memories

of a greater ...contrast of colors
than a black stallion amid
a field of red poppies

of a song that is silkier..
than the melody...of a heart melting
of a mountaintop that is higher..
than the ambitions..in a child's eyes

of something whiter...
than a dove's
angel-kissed feathers

of something warmer,
deeper, richer ....than life's
meaning...embedded within families
friendships, in the histories,
mysteries, unknown to us

of something gentler...
than a mother's touch
upon her baby's forehead...

tell me... if there is...
something more powerful
than the presence
of God...

of something fiercer
than the love with which
i gaze upon you
of something softer ...
than the tenderness
with which i hold you.

To the World

To the world you may just be
a speck ...
of white
but to me,
my kaleidoscope palette,

a fleeting star
in the cosmic ..
scheme of things

to them
you may just be
a single petal

to me,
my entire garden.

Mystical

Love, be
mystical,

as the flickering
blue flame
of night,

as the fully...
awoken moon,
beneath cobwebs
of passing clouds
amidst chanting
high-tides,

fuzzy,
as my blanket,

big enough
to illuminate a hundred
thousand billion galaxies

and just small enough to fit
into my embrace.

Night Soul

I will forever be...
the night-winged soul
lingering beneath
mythical skies...

awaiting the silence
of amber-dark streets
where sanctity flows ...
in the hoot of owls, and
crashing diamonds of tides

watching Arcturus guard
the Little and Great Bear
of the heavens, with twinkling fierceness

dreaming... of Saturn's
62 moons

i will forever be...colliding
with a billion unnamed..
undiscovered stars, each of us
on our own orbital paths

with shadows of flight
criss-crossing the air

savouring the sacred wine
of this hour...this very second
when every flutter

every flicker in the dark
swish in the wind

every ripple, scent
every pulse, every breath
every movement, every stillness

is a poem.

Savoring Poetry

It is to be savored like a
seabreeze-whispered...

dream...in the mysterious
blue minutes...
before dawn

like a secret...
infatuation.... like slow...
languorous sips

of green tea... like a lingering
glimpse... a self-wrapped
paradise...

like his name
upon my lips.

A Normal Life

How can it ever be possible for me
to return to living
a normal life

after having been possessed
in mind and spirit...by the silken
splendor of the moon

after the sweetness
of last week's laughter...
still bubbling over me like
pink champagne

after having swayed ,
with the heart of a child
in a seagull-stirred breeze...

after being soul-awash,
in the breath of tuberoses
and lime blossoms, permanently
tanned, in the summer of poetry,
captivated by the festival
of faces, and family, friendships
and food,

after having my heart
painfully pierced

by starlight
and spring showers

after having been haunted
by the fading piano tunes
of passing days...

how can i ever
breathe...normally again

after having been cradled
by the kind of sorrow
so silent...that it nourishes

after having been swept
by the kind of joy…
so absolute...that it wounds.

Sunday Evenings

There have been endless
Saturdays swaying...
through the languor
of sun-drizzled,
palm tree afternoons

there have been mornings...
so quiet and tender..
like a poem, on Thursday's lips...
that I wondered
if I'd been kissed at all....

there have been dazzling
cascades of Fridays... ornamenting
the Nights with necklaces
of moon and pearls

but it is ...
the Sunday evenings I adore
the most, that bring
all of us together

with my grandfather seated
in his favorite spot, cradling
a frolicking six month old
great-grandchild

amidst long, warm chats,
and a cricket match
running on television, the classic

aromas of Mutton Stew and Kebabs
spicing up the air

along with my aunt,
cousins, and brother...
roaring at something hilarious,
that happened ten years ago

my mother, and grandmother
completing the picture..
even if they weren't
already smiling...

my dad reminiscing his own
time of youth ..out loud

talking of how time
had gone...

how time was always gone
that never waited, nor cared
to pause or explain

and me, in the midst
of it all, quietly cherishing
the Sunday evening, that always meant

so much more…
than celebrating, the festival
of ordinary life.

so fleeting in nature,
so everlasting in spirit.

No Proclamations

There are no proclamations, sometimes

no diamond mandolins flowing....
with melodies of love
nor evening-dew dripping
with rings or sweet nothings...

no embraces...
warm enough

no kisses,
nor poetry...

just a quiet gaze,
from the corner ,that says,

I'll always be here

Just a Smidgen

Leave me just a smidgen
of a rainbow...to remain
besotted with for months,

some jasmine-clouded tea
some sandwiches

and a smile, just warm enough...
to spend a million
golden afternoons in

some family anecdotes,
for the woebegone days,

some of mother's own
brand of laughter,
for the utterly
miserable ones

leave my skies
a shade of heart-stopping blue
along with blown kisses
of white birds

leave me with wings of books,
on the coffee table, some music
that's chocolate for the heart,

some unbreakable spells
of *Downton Abbey*
and some rain-smudged
sunsets by the sea,

some almost-whiffs of poetry...
in the most unexpected places, ...moments

with some aching...
that will only heal...
in the mosque of sleep,

with thunderstorms...
as dear to me,
as the quiet gentleness
of your breath on my cheek.

Walking Tall

(for my grandfather)

His hair still shine...
like a fresh sorbet of snow
with the same white blaze...
of an old family video
from twenty one years ago

he can still...walk tall,
an imposing personality
one that can command respect
with just one stride,

his hands can still endure...
the sweat of hard work,
and juggle time.... with ease,
handle an unruly great-grandchild,
hold and walk his frail wife,
through a crowded
railway station,

with a mind that can still
brave the evening traffic,
and business losses

with a spirit that can still
go river rafting, and mountain
climbing, take bath in waters
below zero degrees

he remains....untouched,
by the wrinkled hands of time
unbeaten...unruffled

with a heart that can still take on
hundred more years of life
as a warrior

and love the same...
all over again, tie a scattered
flower-bunch of families together…
in celebration or tragedy
and make my own heart

glad to be alive in a world where

his gently awakening eyes,
nourish the morning sun.